CLAPHAM THROUGH
TWO CENTURIES

First edition, published in 2001 by

WOODFIELD PUBLISHING
Woodfield House, Babsham Lane, Bognor Regis
West Sussex PO21 5EL, England.

ISBN 1-903953-07-3

Clapham
Through
Two
Centuries

JOHN F. PICKERING

Woodfield Publishing
~ WEST SUSSEX · ENGLAND ~

Contents

Acknowledgements 7

Preface 11

1 ~ Clapham between the late 1700s and 1800s 13

2 ~ Businesses & Occupations Between the 1800s & 1960 21

3 ~ Clapham's Main Employers 37

4 ~ Farming in Clapham 1890 – 1960 57

5 ~ The Boer War 67

6 ~ Facts & Events In Clapham 1800 – Late 1905 68

7 ~ Clapham's King George V Playing Field 97

8 ~ Clapham Club 111

9 ~ Henman's Garage – A Clapham Family Business 115

10 ~ Two Clapham Mysteries 119

11 ~ The Growth of Clapham from the 1950s 121

12 ~ Clapham – A Summary 127

Acknowledgements

I would like to thank the staff of the Archives Department of Bedfordshire County Council for all their help to me in obtaining most of the information in this book on my many visits.

My thanks also go to Clapham Golf Club who allowed me to obtain information from C.W. Hulance's book *The Story of a Golf Club*; Mr Ray Henman who gave me information about Henman's Garage.

Finally, my thanks go to my wife Eileen, who typed and edited the manuscript. I dedicate this book to her.

This old house in the High Street was demolished in the 1970s and the site redeveloped. The butcher's shop on th right was built on the site of an old thatched cottage. Just two of the many changes that have taken place in Clapham in recent years.

List of Illustrations

Tollgate Cottage 16

Woodlands Lodge House 16

Rev Cowburn and ladies of the church c.1900. 19

Clapham Post Office in its present position 20

W. Hewitt's Post Office before it moved 20

Tinsley & Arnold's Dairy delivery Van in the 1920s. 27

Woodlands Manor – then and now. 36

The entrance to Clapham Park. 45

The Manor House, Clapham Park. 45

Convent in Clapham Park grounds. 47

Farming at the turn of the century. 56

The Ford, Clapham. 59

Little Park Farm. 65

The old Ursula Taylor Primary School, built in 1872 71

The new Ursula Taylor Primary School, built in the 1970s. 71

Highbury Grove in the 1930s 87

Clapham's King George V Playing Field 106

The original Henman's Garage in 1927 114

A car belonging to the Henmans in the 1920s 114

The Horse and Groom public house 129

The Swan public house 129

The Star public house 131

The Fox & Hounds public house 131

Thomas á Becket church and churchyard, Clapham. 133

The Old Vicarage 135

Flooding in Clapham High Street, 1998. 136

Aerial view of the flooding in Clapham, 1998. 137

Preface

After tending my parents' grave one day I walked around Clapham churchyard and read some of the names on the graves. I was surprised to see on one of them my namesake - JOHN PICKERING - who died in 1875. This set me wondering about him and his life in Clapham all those years ago.

My next step was to go to the Records Office at County Hall, Bedford, and during many visits there I traced the Pickerings back to the late 18th century.

First I found RICHARD PICKERING who had married SARAH SWEPSON in 1791. From the four sons they had - RICH, WILLIAM, JOHN and THOMAS, I found that my line was descended from THOMAS. It was his brother JOHN who was buried in the grave that had started me off with my research about the Pickerings of Clapham.

I must confess that the research has almost become an obsession with me and at times it has been very frustrating as there is very little recorded about the village of Clapham. Every time I have found a little snippet of information I have been very elated.

The following is the fruits of my research from the late 18th century to today.

~ 1 ~

Clapham between the
late 1700s and 1800s

IN THE LATE 1700S CLAPHAM CONSISTED of three farms
and fifteen small cottages which were scattered about the
village. The farms that were in Clapham in 1793 were
Church Farm, Green Farm (or Park Farm as we now
know it) and Little Park Farm, which is in Clapham Park.

The fifteen cottages were mostly in the High Street
(or the High Road as it was then called). There were also
about five or six in Green Lane.

There was also 'The Horse and Jockey' (licensed in
1705) — now called 'The Horse and Groom'.

Most of the really old cottages, especially the ones in
Green Lane, were demolished in the 1800s as most of
them were agricultural labourers' cottages which were
only two-bedroomed, cramped and draughty dwellings. A

government survey recommended that a third of all agricultural houses in Great Britain should be demolished and rebuilt, as most had stood since the Middle Ages. A few more houses were then built in the village during the 1880s.

Some of the oldest cottages are still around, for example the thatched cottage on the Clapham boundary and the small row of cottages opposite the Post Office, which are the oldest in the High Street.

The thatched cottage on the Clapham boundary was at one time the coachman's cottage to Woodlands Manor. The entrance was through a large white gate which can still be seen. The gravel road curved round to the back of the Manor. It was in the 1890s that my grandfather was the head coachman to the Woodlands Manor, and lived in this thatched cottage with his large family. My father was born there in 1892, also my aunt.

Inside the cottage there was a living room, a small kitchen and just two bedrooms. With small cottages and large families of the day, people now can hardly imagine where they put them all in such cramped conditions!

The cottage also had a cellar. Lighting was by candles, later it had oil lamps. Heating was by a large coal-fired range with a boiler at the side to heat the water. The toilet was drained to a cesspool at the bottom of the garden for there was no mains water on in those days of course. Water was obtained from a deep well.

My grandfather had other duties to attend to around the estate, as well as looking after the horses and keeping the carriage spotlessly clean. My grandmother during this time was a needlewoman and lace-maker.

The oldest parts of Clapham are Green Lane (known as The Green in the 1700s and 1800s); The Warren, which has at least one house which was built in 1878 (the row of cottages at the top of The Warren are called 'The Leys Cottages'); and Preservine Walk, with houses dated 1885 with two much older, smaller cottages in the middle of one row.

The old stone cottage on the corner of Green Lane was at one time the lodge house to the Woodlands Manor. Opposite, next to The Ford, stood an old

Tollgate Cottage

*The Woodlands Lodge House at the
corner of Green Lane and the High Street.*

thatched cottage which was known as Tollgate Cottage, now demolished and houses built on the site.

With so few buildings around during this time of the early 19th century, the church must have looked an awesome sight, dominating the skyline as it did.

One of the oldest houses in Clapham is the old farmhouse at Park Farm in Green Lane. It was probably built in the sixteenth or seventeenth century and at one time it was known as Green Farm. It has a long history to it; some say that there is a ghost in the place and it has a secret room which hid a Cavalier from the Roundheads.

There were one or two cottages at the Folly end of the village but they are sadly no longer there.

Jesse Katharine Haddock bequeathed the Reading Room at the top of The Warren to the village in her will dated 1917, but was actually built between 1898 and 1900 on land sold for building in 1898. The building is no longer used and is now dilapidated.

There used to be a very old cottage close to where the reservoir is along Bedford Road. I have seen a photograph of it with one of my old aunts sitting in the doorway with her lace-making pillow. Next to this cottage was an old barn, known as the Red Barn because of the red pantiles on the roof. Both fell into disrepair and were demolished, probably in the 1950s. There is part of a brick building still standing which was used for stabling a horse.

During and just before the twentieth century a lot of the fields around Clapham had names to them. The fields near to Highbury Grove were known as Little Grove, Great Grove and Coney Grove. From the Allotments up to where Milton Road starts, the fields were known as Great, East and Middle Carol. Those at the top half were known as Crowhills, and went up to Twinwoods. In the fields near to Clapham Hospital those fields were known as Gravel Close. In the Oakley Road turn, on top of Milton Hill was, and still is, a large spinney known as Judge's Spinney.

In the early 1900s there was a large spinney known as Crabtree, which was close to and at the back of a farm known as Rookery Farm, the farmer being a Mr Edward Joseph Stratford. It stood behind the Woodlands Manor

House, the resident at the manor at this time was a Mr William Fitzpatrick.

In the early 1900s the river was more prominent and could be seen nearly all the way through the village. In the spring it would mostly be in flood, especially after a heavy fall of snow, and in some years it would flood the High Street to quite a depth.

The Rev Cowburn and ladies of the church outside the Reading Room c.1900.

Clapham Post Office (above) in its present position. Previous site next door with Preservine Walk in between.
(Bedfordshire County Archives)

W. Hewitt's Post Office before it moved to the opposite side of Preservine Walk. The building became a bakery and is now a Pizza Restaurant.
(Bedfordshire County Archives)

~ 2 ~

Businesses & Occupations Between the 1800s & 1960

In the late 1890s Clapham had a blacksmith named Ebenezer Jordon. His smithy stood on the site where the Q8 garage is today (run by Mr Colin Henman) and backed onto the river. I suppose with farms having several shire horses, he had quite a good trade, but according to the 1906 Kelly's Directory, the blacksmith was no longer trading. After it closed down it must have gone through some sort of conversion for in 1919 there was only a cottage owned by Mr Henry Jaques, called 'The Smithy'.

It was during the late 1800s and early 1900s that one of my ancestors, William Pickering, was a carter in the village. He lived with his wife and family in London Row (The Terrace) in the High Street. He carried mostly beer gasses and other materials for public houses. His son, also named William, was his assistant. He also employed another man to help him out. He rented some land in Bromham for his horse to graze and to store his cart. His daughter, who in 1891 was fifteen years old, was working as a kitchen maid at Woodlands Manor. His other son, eleven year old Philip, was working as an agricultural worker on the Woodlands estate during this time.

When I look at the history of Clapham, I find that the name of Pickering has been associated with the village for well over two hundred years. As stated in the previous chapter, my father was born in the coachman's cottage of Woodland's Manor, his father being the head coachman. My mother was born in Luton in 1893, although she was Christened in Clapham Church. Her father was born in Clapham but through his work in the building trade as a skilled bricklayer, he moved around a little, to where there was work. He and his wife and children moved back to Clapham in the 1900s.

In the 1901 census there were just 788 people living in the now thriving village.

A wheelwright lived in the village by the name of Charles Poole. I should imagine he made a good living both making and repairing wheels for the local farmers' carts, wheelbarrows and pony traps.

Opposite the Warren stood a laundry, which was owned by a Mrs Clara Swann. Before the First World War, a Mr Frederick Tinsley, who was not only the Parish Council Clerk, but also the local undertaker in the village, had his workshop at the laundry premises, after it had moved. He later used the building next to the Methodist chapel (built around 1920) as a workshop. Later it was used by the British Legion, for local gatherings and a child clinic.

In around 1901, two unmarried sisters, Sarah and Emma Mays, owned a drapery and grocers shop in Clapham.

A few of the village women were prominent in the making of pillow lace, which was quite a business around 1906. It must have been hard on their eyes for houses only had oil lamps for lighting.

In the early 1900s Mr William Prentice was a small farmer and his brother Walter was also a carter.

There was a boot and shoemaker's business on the corner of The Close (where 'Charlies' is today). It was owned by Mr Alfred Mathews who could also mend watches as well. His brother, Mr Thomas Mathews, was a shoemaker, but was also the proprietor of the village Post Office.

Another shoe repairer around 1906 was a Mr Joseph Flavell.

In 1910, among the seven or eight farms around Clapham, was Mount Pleasant Farm, where the farmer was a Mr Thomas Clark. He certainly believed in diversification for he was not only a farmer, but also a patent boot and shoe tree manufacturer. In those days the leather was not very pliable so the boots or shoes needed to be stretched or kept in shape. Who would have thought that in that day and age, that two entirely different occupations could have been carried out in a village like Clapham!

Around 1910 there was a Mr Frederick Walter Waller who was a fruit grower and florist. He made wreaths and crosses to order and also specialised in bedding plants, tomatoes and chrysanthemums.

Also around at this time was a Miss Ada Facey, a dressmaker who lived in the High Street.

During and just after the 1914-18 war, a Mr John Pettit ran the Post Office, which then stood on the site where the pizza restaurant is today. In the 1920s he was also a baker, grocer and tobacconist plus a corn and provision merchant. Not content with all these occupations, he was also a District Councillor. Quite a busy man! His brother, Roland, was the Clerk to the Parish Council.

In the early years of the 1900s, Mr Thomas Dawson was the local jobbing bricklayer of the village, who lived in The Warren. A Wilfred Dawson was also a jobbing bricklayer.

By 1914 and through the First World War, there were several women of the village who made pillow lace for a living. This craft went on well into the 1920s. The lace was collected from the lace-makers and sold to Braggins. Because the shop gave the workers so little for all their hard work, the lace-makers began to use a bobbin or two less on each item so they could make it more worth their while. Although this system no longer operates, there are still several lacemakers still in the village who do it for their own pleasure to this day.

In 1924 there was a Mr Walter Tysoe who was a plumber and glazier, who lived in the High Street.

Mr Percy Pfau was a carpenter. His workshop was next to The Terrace. I well remember him many years later riding around on a motorbike with a wooden sidecar (made by himself no doubt) and painted the same colour green as his workshop.

It wasn't until about 1926 that a grocer, Mr William Hewitt, moved to the Post Office. By 1928 the Post Office moved premises to where it is today, on the other side of Preservine Walk. Mr William J. Bryant took over the former Post Office building and land behind it and carried on the bakery business, making and selling bread, cakes and buns. The ovens were coal-fired and steam piped.

Frederick Poole was still going strong, working as a wheelwright at the Folly end of the village.

Also around 1928 a Mr John R. Pyper ran a florists at a place known as 'Ousebank'.

There were two dairymen around – Tinsley and Arnold, who ran the Park Farm Dairy in Green Lane.

Mrs Louisa Humes was running a small grocery store which stood at the bottom corner of The Warren (now a Chinese Takeaway).

Tinsley & Arnold's Dairy delivery Van in the 1920s.

In the late 1920s Clapham had its most popular and best known District Nurse whose name was Eva Wilson. She was not just a nurse, but a midwife as well. She was kept very busy bringing a number of babies into the world, including both my wife and myself. She lived in the High Street opposite The Warren. You would often see her around at all hours in her matron-style uniform, either walking or riding her bicycle. She was a great character of the village and died sometime in the 1950s.

As we entered the 1930s, Charles Franklin still ran the brickyards along Clapham Road, although by now it was mostly rundown, for now he was more into coal.

Also in the 1930s there was a grocery shop at the Folly end of the village which was owned by a Mrs Emily Brown.

Mrs Clara Swann was still at the Laundry in the High Street, but shortly after it changed hands. The new owners were Bray and Baker.

By 1931 the population of the village was 811 – it hadn't grown much in thirty years.

In the middle 1930s things started to pick up after the war and the Depression. It was during this time that Mr Herbert Dawson opened his greengrocery shop in the High Street. It was a small shop, the premises are still there to this day, next to Alan Sturgess the Travel Agents. Bert Dawson ran the shop with his wife. They lived in Milton Road.

Mr Percy Dawson started his bakery business. It stood behind his house in the High Street, just by 'Riverside'. He used to deliver bread around the village in a van and his brother rode a bicycle with a large bread basket on the front of it. Baker Dawson was around until about the late 1950s.

There was a cobbler in the village in the 1930s, a Mr Frederick Hodby who repaired boots and shoes, and worked in his wooden workshop which he had built himself. It was on the end of his old pantiled cottage which stood just behind 'The Fox and Hounds' Public House in Oakley Road. Fred Hodby was a very good cobbler, he used only the best leather, and did all the stitching of boots and shoes by hand. He repaired many a shoe for my family, and my wife's as well over the years. At one time Fred used to go to the Carlton Reform School for Boys and teach them his cobbler skills. He was a wonderful old chap and a great character. He died in 1979 at the ripe old age of 92 years. I don't think Clapham has had a cobbler since then.

At 69 High Street Mr Percy Felts was a grocer around 1936. He was also a tea dealer.

There was also a small café known as 'The Orchard Tea Rooms' owned by a Mr Thody at the Folly end of the village in the High Street. The tea rooms were in a wooden building (next to what is now the Folly Stores Spar shop). The building is still there to this day but has been converted into a small bungalow. In those days, where the caravan site is now, most of the ground was an orchard (hence the name 'Orchard' tea rooms.)

Clapham also had a horse riding school, owned by Miss Joan Tinsley, eldest daughter of Mr Percy Tinsley. It was in Green Lane and stood in the grounds of Park Farm and backed onto the old farmhouse. The school was taken over when Mrs Joan Bayliss, as she became, had a fall and retired. The stables are still there to this day. They were originally built in 1873.

There was also another dairy farmer in the village. This dairy belonged to a Mr Walter Prentice who delivered most of his milk by pony and trap.

It was during the 1940s that a large gravel pit, which was at the Folly end of the village, was started. It was run by 'The Clapham Sand and Gravel Company'.

There were quite a few small businesses up at the Folly and Milton Road end of Clapham at this time. Next to the gravel pit was another Riding School. This was run by a Mr J.B. Stopps and known as the Clapham Riding School.

Further up the village in Milton Road, just next to the Hospital, was 'Oak-Lea' Dog Kennels, owned in the 1940s by Mr P.E. Flemons.

Another boarding kennels were the 'Hillside Kennels' which were at the bottom of Milton Hill. They were owned by Mr Wickens-Smith.

It was during the war years that there was a butcher's shop owned by Mr Cyril Huckvale. The shop is still there, but it is the Allen Sturgess Travel shop now. During the war Cyril joined the army and while he was away on war service, his shop was run by his wife and a Mr Ted Quince. In fact it was during this time that the shop was in two halves; one half the butchery and the other was a grocery store. The grocery was run by Mr Ron Hewitt and his wife, Pearl. I remember going in the grocery part of the shop quite often for my mother. On one occasion I can remember asking for Farmers Glory – a cereal like cornflakes. I have often wondered what happened to that cereal. I think it was just a wartime commodity. Ron's mother, Mrs Hewitt, ran the Clapham Post Office at this time.

In the High Street, opposite Highbury Grove, was a hairdresser's run by a Mr E.S. Robinson.

Clapham in the early 1940s had three Garages. One was run by Mr Frederick Sparrow. He owned several lorries which mostly carried sand and gravel, and other materials. I used to have a ride sometimes when the driver was out on a delivery – something that would never be allowed today!

Next door to Sparrow's stood an old, dilapidated house with white painted walls, although most of it was covered in ivy. In front of the house stood about five very tall poplar trees which used to swing about in the wind. Next to the old house stood another Garage, and still does. In the late 1920s George Henman repaired bicycles and motorcycles, then with the motorcar more on the streets, his son Harold joined him and they repaired them and sold petrol. It is now run by one of Harold's sons, Colin and the Garage is now called the Q8 garage. More of this family business in a later chapter.

The next Garage is at the Folly end of the village and was then called 'The Reliance Garage' run by Saysell & Gower in the late 1920s to the mid 1930s, then E.A. Thompson took it over. Mr Thompson was also a Special Constable. In later years it was run by his daughter and son-in-law, Mr Richards, then his grandson, Rod, took up the reins, and today it is known as 'Thompson's Garage'. They no longer sell petrol, but repair and sell cars.

In 1927, Mr David Brown had quite a large house built. It stood at the Folly end of the village, near to the

Oakley turn. He later bought a large wooden hut and started a shop, until the 1930s. After he died, his wife, Mrs Emily Brown, added another storey to the house, then used one of the downstairs rooms as a shop. It became known as Brown's Stores, a general grocery and tobacconist. Mrs Brown served in the shop throughout the war years and after. It was after the war when it was known as the Folly Stores, that her son, Arthur, took over the shop. During this time it was enlarged once again, making it a really spacious shop. In later years after Arthur died, his son, David, took over and it is still going strong today, but is known as the Spar Shop.

It was in the late thirties that Browns began their Caravan Park business, which was built on an old orchard. Today it has grown to form a large mobile home park, and is certainly part of the Clapham Folly scene.

There is another shop at the Folly end of the village that stands near to Mount Pleasant corner. The shop has been there since the early 1930s. Although it has changed hands on several occasions, I do remember it was once owned by Knowltons during the 1940s and 1950s. Nowadays it had become a mini supermarket shop.

During the Second World Wartime years and just after, opposite the Swan Public House was a Mr Charles Purslow, who ran a plumbing and glazing business.

In the Milton Road end of the village, we now have the Texaco Garage, which has been there since the 1970s. It not only sells petrol, but also has a mini market and car washing facilities. It is built on the old entrance to the site of the old sand pit.

Mr Thomas Dawson, who lived in The Warren, was the local bricklayer and odd-job man. He used to do quite a bit of work around the village right up to the early 1960s.

Woodlands Manor – then and now.

3

Clapham's Main Employers

1 ~ WOODLANDS MANOR

One of Clapham's employers was the Woodlands Estate. In 1812 John Thomas Dawson sold property in Yorkshire and bought land, in all 136 acres, which included Rookery Farm, a cottage and a carpenter's cottage on part of Picketts and Crabtree Close from Lord Ashburnham.

John Thomas Dawson had Woodlands Manor built in Green Lane and lived there for the first four years from 1813-1816. He had lived in a large house in St. Paul's Square since 1802.

J.T. Dawson was married to Mary and they had a son, John Frederick, born in 1803, and a daughter, Ellen, born in 1816.

From around 1817 Woodlands was let to a Thomas Addington and later a Thomas Green.

J.T. Dawson's eldest son, John Frederick, married Hester Wade in 1827. J.F. was at Trinity College at age 18. He was ordained Deacon in 1826 and became incumbent of two parishes in Lincoln; Rector of St. Peters, Toynton and Vicar of All Saints, also in Toynton from 1827 until his death in 1870. He was also the author of *Popular Illustrations of Remarkable Events in the New Testament* (Crockford).

The Reverend J.F. Dawson and his wife Hester had two children, Ada Elizabeth and William Henry.

In 1830 J.T. Dawson became Bedford's High Sheriff. His wife, Mary, died in 1837 and he followed her in 1850 on 27th September, aged 69.

The Reverend John Frederick Dawson was by now 47 when he inherited Woodlands estates. He leased cottages in The Warren, two lodges, farms, land at Riverside, cottages at Roadside, Tollgate Cottage, and a cottage at The Green.

Hester and John Frederick's son, William Henry, was apparently a very sickly child who had not been expected to live long. He was not, therefore, taught to read and write until he was around 21 years old.

After William Henry's mother died in 1860, aged 54, his father, the Reverend Dawson remarried two years later to his housekeeper, the 23 year old Alice Proctor.

In 1864 the Reverend Dawson started his second family with the birth of a son, also named John Frederick. In 1866 a daughter was born, Alice Mary, and in 1869 Eleanor Caroline was born. A year later, the Reverend Dawson died in October 1870, aged 67. During the last years of his life he was away from Woodlands and the manor was let to William Shilleto. It was later let to the Fitzpatrick Family.

It came as a big disappointment, and probably even shock to William Henry Dawson to discover that his father, the Reverend John Frederick Dawson had left everything to the son of his second family (also named John Frederick), now only six years old. William Henry had only been left an annuity of £200. He went off to live on the Isle of Wight. He would at least have liked to have lived on the Woodlands Estate, at Rookery Farm, but this was already let to a George Ballingall and legal proceedings to get him evicted proved unsuccessful and costly.

There had been rumours that the Reverend Dawson had made a previous will, leaving everything to William, and encouraged by a solicitor, Alfred Nicholson, William's representatives applied to the Home Secretary to have the Reverend Dawson's coffin exhumed. This was mainly on the evidence of a carpenter from Gwyn Street, Bedford who had sealed down the coffin and said there had been papers put inside it. So on this man's word, permission was granted and in October 1876, the Reverend Dawson's extremely well-preserved body was exhumed and a bundle of papers was found. These were far less well preserved than the Reverend, being stained and falling to pieces, but it was established that they were not legal documents, but letters from the Reverend's first wife, Hester.

What a terrible disappointment this must have been for William who had heard from various people, including the Rector of Bletsoe, that there had been another will. If there had, it was never found.

In 1890, William Long Fitzpatrick took on the estate. He was not only the Chairman of the Clapham Parish Council, but a Justice of the Peace, and in 1905 he became High Sheriff of Bedfordshire.

It was the Fitzpatricks who my grandfather worked for as head coachman. Woodlands also employed others of my relations over the years as domestics or farm labourers.

My grandfather also had two groomsmen working with him. The men and their families had to bow and curtsy to the Fitzpatricks, and my grandfather had to make sure he was well turned out in his white trousers (jodhpurs), high black boots, and his black frock coat with his high silk hat. The Fitzpatricks would often go to Colmworth House in Sharnbrook by carriage, and my grandfather would have to sit and wait, in all weathers, until the Fitzpatricks wanted to return to Woodlands Manor.

Around the time of the Fitzpatricks, Edward Joseph Stratford was the farmer on the adjoining Rookery Farm. It was only a few years after this that no trace of Rookery Farm appears on any map.

By 1920 a Richard Allen was at the Woodlands. From 1924 the Manor was unoccupied until around 1927 when Major General Sir Percy and Lady Cox took over.

During this occupancy, the Coxes held various sales of furniture and bric-a-brac to help with the upkeep of the place. In an account in the Bedfordshire Times, Sir Percy was portrayed as rather a hero. He was a prominent member of the Oakley Hunt and one day, whilst riding between Oakley and Stevington, a woman came off her horse into the river. Sir Percy walked in up to his neck and rescued her. Apparently she was not badly hurt. It was shortly after this incident that because Lady Cox was suffering with ill health, they decided to move to London.

During the Second World War Woodlands was taken over by the War Ministry and was run as a boarding house. Sir Adrian Boult lived there for some time during the war as there were quite a few recordings made at the Corn Exchange, where Glenn Miller also recorded.

In the late 1950s and 1960s Woodlands was owned by the Staveley Industries Group, a research group for machine tools. Fifty people worked there, twenty five of which were graduates.

After this Woodlands Manor became a hotel and restaurant and a good venue for functions, and is doing well in the year 2001.

2 ~ CLAPHAM PARK ESTATE

Clapham Park Manor was completed in 1873 for the sum of £17,000 for James Howard. John Usher was the architect and Fosters of Kempston were the builders. It was John Usher's last assignment before he retired. It was also the grandest house he had worked on, and the only country house.

On the opening day a large gathering of prominent people had arrived for the opening ceremony, which was followed by speeches and a dinner party. It was during the dinner that the 1st Beds Rifle Volunteers played music to help with the celebration.

Clapham Park Estate included Park Farm, Green Farm, College Farm and eight cottages.

James Howard was the owner of Britannia Iron Works in Bedford. He also experimented with different types of farming machinery, including steam engines for ploughing which he had made for working on his estate. His farm was used for scientific purposes, experimenting with sugar beet and other types of crops.

Besides the employees on his farms, records show that in the 1890s James Howard's head coachman was Henry Jackson, who did domestic duties as well. He lived at the coachman's house. The head gardener at this time was Arthur Groom who lived at the gardener's lodge in Clapham Park. The butler at the Manor was William Pollard who also did domestic work. Pollard's son, also named William, was a gardener's assistant, aged just 13 years old. The laundress at the Manor then was a Miss Elizabeth Hunter who was 70. No pension in those days!

The entrance to Clapham Park.

The Manor House, Clapham Park.

In 1889, after James Howard had died, the Manor and Clapham Park came up for auction, but after two months it was reclaimed by the Howards.

James Howard's son, John, who lived at the Manor House after his death, was the founder of Howards of Bedford, who not only made ploughs, but also other farm implements. One of the ploughs stood on top of a shop in Bedford High Street, opposite St. Paul's Square.

The estates remained in the Howards' hands until the late 1930s.

Convent in Clapham Park grounds.

During the last war of 1939-45, it became a rehabilitation centre for the Forces, and then served as a Convalescent Home for Manor House until 1958. Then it became the British Provincial Headquarters for the Daughters of the Holy Ghost Teaching Order of Nuns. 'The Nunnery' as it came to be known, was there until 1985, when it was sold. It has since been resold for development, with some selective houses being built in and around the Park and the Manor itself converted into luxury flats.

The only other large house in Clapham to match Clapham Park Manor House in the early years was the large lodge house at the Folly. Today it is converted into self-contained, warden-controlled flats for the elderly.

3 ~ CLAPHAM GOLF COURSE

In the early 1900s the farmer at Green Farm (renamed Park Farm in the 1930s) was Mr Lancelot Clark. In his spare time he would invite some of his friends over, and they would knock a few golf balls around in a small field.

When he wasn't knocking balls around, he would keep sheep in the field for grazing, but it was still a little rough. As the years went by, enthusiasm increased and additional fields were added.

By 1912, Lancelot Clark, along with his friends, formed a Golf Club. A year later a wooden clubhouse was erected and an eighteen-hole golf course had taken shape. Mr E.J. Tarling was the first secretary, and a Mr G. Muggleton was appointed as the first Professional. That's how the Bedford & County Golf Club was formed.

The head green-keeper was a Mr William (Bill) Loak, who was also responsible for maintenance of the course. Unfortunately the 1914-18 War intervened, with very little golf played.

In the early 1920s, the head green-keeper, Bill Loak, had help with the mowing from some farm labourers from Park Farm. In those days shire-horses were used to pull the large gang-mowers, but they found that the horses' hooves cut up the fairway. A solution was found by strapping on leather shoes to the horses' ankles. The greens were cut by pushing hand mowers. It was hard work and labour intensive.

Bill Loak remained in charge for fourteen years until 1926. He left to take up the post of groundsman and steward at Bedford Bowling Club. Bill lived with his wife, daughter and three sons in a farm cottage adjacent to the course.

During this time in the 1920s, because there were not many golf courses in and around the Home Counties, the Club was known as the Mid-Bedfordshire Golf Club. The Club had built up quite a large membership by this time, having risen to well over 300. In 1922 another golf course had been constructed near Biggleswade, and this one was known as the Mid-Beds Golf Club, so this caused some confusion. It was then decided that the Clapham Club should change its name to the Bedford & County Golf Club, as it is known to this day.

It was during the late 1920s that the committee were determined that water would be provided to the eighteen greens and water amenities to the clubhouse. The

Clapham Golf Club was the only one around by a long way to have such facilities.

In 1925 farming had gone into severe recession, and Lancelot Clark was declared bankrupt. This put the Golf Club in jeopardy, but fortunately a local solicitor, a Mr A. Morrison, purchased the farm and golf course. In 1926 he formed a new Club and made it into a limited company, with seven directors and ten shareholders.

Captain Alfred Pickering RN (retired) [no relation to me] was the secretary in the first years. He became a great stalwart of the Club, and remained as secretary for ten years until 1936, when ill health forced his resignation.

The Club was run by a committee appointed by the members, which included two Lords of the Realm, in Lord Ampthill and Lord St John of Bletsoe. There were also many eminent visitors to the Club, including the Prince of Wales who played the course on several occasions during the late 1920s. Later, of course, he was to become King Edward VIII.

After the departure of Bill Loak, Mr Jack Simons was then appointed head green-keeper, having worked on the course since a boy. He lived in the green-keeper's cottage in the grounds of the Golf Club, his wife becoming the stewardess of the club-house. She became famous for her home-made teas of cakes and scones.

In those early years most golf clubs were hand made by the Professional in his workshop, who was just as much a craftsman as he was a skilful player. Most clubs at this time were hickory-shafted.

The majority of the members in the early days played in jackets and plus-fours (long, wide knickerbockers, so named because to produce the overhang, the length was normally increased by four inches) – very different from the trendy clothes of today's players.

Being a caddie at this time was a popular job for many boys and men of the village. The fees in those days were 1s.6d (7½p) for men and 1/- (5p) for boys per round. If the member felt generous, they would get a gratuity of 1d to 3d (1p) sometimes and especially on Match days, when the caddie would have to carry two sets of clubs, one on each shoulder – no wheels around in those days!

Another job for the caddie was to tee up the ball. This was done by making a pyramid of sand. This went on for quite a while before the tee pegs came along. The sand was in sand boxes at the side of every tee. The caddies came under the responsibility of the Professional, and his instructions had to be obeyed to the letter. If the caddie couldn't locate a missing ball, then he was in trouble. Nevertheless, a lot of Clapham men and boys took the job on, and enjoyed what they were doing, despite the low pay.

The 1920s and 1930s were prosperous times for the Club as membership rose, but somehow the Club was unable to make a profit. Jack Simons had a staff of six men who kept the greens and fairway in immaculate condition right up to the war years.

When war was declared in 1939 there was an immediate ban put on spectator sport, although it didn't affect golf. It was the impact of petrol rationing, and mobilisation into the Forces that took its toll on the Golf

Club. The Club closed down completely in the September of 1942 until after the war.

After the war the directors decided that golf should resume, despite the austerity of the time, and after some laborious work by the greenkeeper, Mr Jack Simons, and his assistants, within six months golf was once again being played at Clapham, the members playing a nine hole course twice.

The first Captain of the Club after the war was Mr Laurie Hall, who lived locally. It was during these first years after the war that one of the rooms of Jack Simons' small cottage was used as a clubhouse, mainly for a changing room and the storage of clubs and shoes.

In 1947, Mr F.P. Tinsley, the farmer at Park Farm, purchased the course from Mr A. Morrison. It took until 1952 before the eighteen hole course was ready for playing, and with the clubhouse restored, Mrs Jack Simons, the stewardess, was offering good beer along with sausage and mash. Dai Rees came and opened the course and the Club was back on its feet.

The 1950s and 1960s were prosperous times for the Club, with extensions to the clubhouse and the planting of trees. The junior golf section was increasing, which the Club had encouraged over the years, and during this time the Club professional was John MacDonald, who went on to play the international circuit.

It was also a sad time, for in 1966, Jack Simons, the long-time head greenkeeper died. His wife had died a few years earlier. Mel Labram, Jack's assistant for many years, was immediately appointed to the job, and was the head greenkeeper for over thirty years until his retirement. It is a marvellous achievement for the Club that there have been just three greenkeepers in all of those years since the golf course was formed in 1912.

Throughout the 1970s and 1980s, more changes were made to the clubhouse as membership was increasing, with both the men and the ladies. The Professional during these years was Mr Eddie Bullock, who had been with the Club since 1977. After making the move to Club Manager, he then moved to take up the post of Manager at Woburn Golf and Country Club.

Into the 1990s the Club was in a sound financial position now and it was decided to extend the sprinkler system to all the tees. Every tee throughout the course now had a sprinkler. Other projects followed, such as new parking facilities and toilet facilities by the eleventh tee. All ambitious projects which could only have been dreamed about by those early stalwarts of times past. Lancelot Clark certainly started something when he began knocking a few golf balls about some ninety-odd years ago!

The Bedford and County Golf Club must be proud of the generations of past members for the marvellous clubhouse and its facilities, and the wonderful course. The people of Clapham should be very proud to have such a splendid Golf Club in the village.

I have mentioned some of the past members' names but it is not possible to mention them all.

My thanks go to the author C.W. Hulance, who wrote such a splendid book, *The Story of a Golf Club*, from which I obtained much of the foregoing information.

Farming at the turn of the century.

4

Farming in Clapham
1890 – 1960

Agriculture has always been prominent in the village and the farmers employed quite a number of the local people. Many of my ancestors were agricultural labourers. In the early days workers had to be good, all-round skilled workers. Horses did most of the heavy work, and had to be cared for, as of course the traction engine hadn't arrived on the scene by then, and all operations on the farm had to be done by hand. There was the cattle and sheep to tend to and certain labourers specialised in animal husbandry.

Henry George Belgrave was the farmer at Little Park Farm in the late 1890s, in the grounds of Clapham Park. The heavy work such as ploughing was done by the Shire Horse with a labourer walking behind the plough, ensuring that the furrow was as straight as possible. The horse came into its own at harvest time, with the labourer behind the binder, the farm hands picking up the sheaves and putting them into shocks. It was hard and dusty work, especially after taking the horse and cart loaded with hay back to the farm, to the thresher where it was thrown up to the labourers on top of the hayrick. The hours worked were long, and the work was hard.

The only water for the animals was from ponds in the fields, and after a hot, dry summer when the ponds had dried up, the labourer would have to go to the Ford and get water from the river in buckets and fill the tank on the cart. This had to be done at least five or six times a day.

At that time the farm labourer worked for very little reward, for the wages at the beginning of the 20th century were less than a £1 a week. Children as young as 11 years were also working on the land, as labourers or in domestic work in the farm houses and the big estate houses. They worked throughout their lives for very little reward, some were still working aged 70 if they were well enough for there was no retirement age and no pension. Most lived in tied cottages and one wonders where they went when their working life was over. A lot of the women tried to make more money if they could by doing needlework, lace-making or rug making out of rags. Some took in washing. It was hard at times in those 'good old days'!

In the early 1900s the population of the village at this time was around seven hundred, with most of the men working on the land.

The Ford, Clapham.

According to the Agricultural Census of 1901, Clapham consisted of 1995 acres, of which 789 acres, or three quarters, was arable land.

The farms that were about at this time were Outfield Farm, which stood on the Clapham/Ravensden border, the farmer being a Mr John Howkins.

Littlewood Farm stood near to the Oakley Little Wood, which was on the Thurleigh border, the farmer was a Mr Frederick Howkins.

The farmer at Mount Pleasant Farm was a Mr Thomas Clark.

Twinwood Farm, which stood near to a large wood of the same name, was farmed by a Mr Frank Kidman.

College Farm stood right in the middle of fields, they make up the golf course today. It also had a large pond near to it which came from a spring. The farmer in the 1900s was a Mr Lancelot Clark.

Park Farm, which was also known as Green Farm at one time, was also owned by Mr Lancelot Clark, the farmer who started the Golf Club.

Little Park Farm stood in the middle of Clapham Park, and was surrounded at one time by the Clapham Park wood. It also had a large pond surrounded by trees and shrubbery near by. The farmer was a Mr Alfred Fuller.

Another farm, situated along the Bedford Road, opposite to where the Waterworks is today, was a dairy farm, owned by Mr William Prentice.

Three quarters of the farmland around Clapham was arable, and the crops that were mostly grown were barley, wheat and corn with some peas and beans.

It was not until the late 1920s that the tractor began to take the place of the Shire horses, but until then, there was plenty of work for the farm labourers. At harvest time the crops were cut by the binder, drawn by Shire horse, and the same at ploughing time with the farm labourer walking many miles behind the plough.

The average wage for a farm labourer in 1906 was between twelve and eighteen shillings a week, (or sixty to ninety pence in today's money). Some had quite large families to keep, feed and clothe, and it makes you wonder just how they managed.

Church Farm still used Shire horses to do most of the hard work, even in the 1920s. The farm consisted of about five hundred acres. Mr Harold Rush was the farmer at the time. There were also some forty to fifty milking cows on the farm that had to be milked twice a day.

The tractor wasn't invented until 1902. One of the first tractors was the 'Ivel' which was invented by a Bedfordshire man, a Mr Dan Albone who came from Biggleswade. He was giving demonstrations around various farms at this time. By 1904, mowers, reapers, and the binder were improved so that they could be attached to tractors. There was the odd tractor around the farms of Clapham just before the First World War. The tractor began doing the ploughing and was used more at harvest time though, but before the tractor and reaper could start to cut the harvest, a labourer had to go round with a hand scythe and cut a track, just the same as he had to with the horses. Afterwards the sheaves had to be picked up by hand and stood up into shocks, for there was no combine harvester around then.

Shire horses were still used during and after the Second World War. I well remember the farm labourers used to let us young boys lead the horse and cart to and from the farm.

In the 1940s, there was a poultry farmer at the Folly end of the village named Mr William Wooltorton.

In the war years of 1939 and '40, the Church Farm had acquired another owner. This time it was run by Captain Gordon Muirhead, with his wife and daughter. The large farmhouse had a long gravel driveway from the High Street. You entered through a large five-bar farm gate. The drive ran into a circle at the front of the house so that a pony and trap (later motor cars) could turn round without backing. The house and grounds were surrounded by a stone wall, which is still there today. The house also had four or five Scots Pine trees in front of it and an iron fence and gate that enclosed the house and garden. There was also a small wooden gate in the grounds, which led to the church. The gate is still there to this day. At the back of the house was a small orchard of both cooking and eating apples. The Muireheads sold a lot of the apples while they lived there. The large field in the front was mostly used to graze horses, and sometimes the odd fete was held there.

In the 1950s Church Farmhouse reverted to a rented property, owned by Mrs Molly Barcock, daughter of Mr Percy Tinsley. Mr and Mrs Wesley lived there at this time, and did so until the 1970s, when the house was demolished. An archaeological 'dig' took place there. They did not find much except for the remains of three previous old Manor Houses and a rounded dovecote, also some dog skeletons and wild boar bones, but nothing exciting was found. After the dig, the site was cleared and the new Ursula Taylor Primary School was built. The old school which was built in 1872, was demolished to make way for new houses.

The farmer at the Mount Pleasant Farm in the 1940s was Mr Cyril Flanders. The land stretched from the old George Street, up to Twinwoods.

There was another poultry farm in the village which was in the grounds called Fairfield, at Twinwoods. It was known as Spriggs Poultry Farm, owned by Mr R. Spriggs. It was the highest farmland in Clapham. In the 1960s it was the only pre-war accredited poultry breeding station in the County still functioning. The breeding stock of over 500 were kept under free-range. There was also a battery house for egg production, having over 900 pullets. Pedigree Anglo-Nubian goats were kept for breeding.

In the 1960s the three farms of Park, Church and College, employed 12 men and consisted of cattle,

Little Park Farm.

including an Angus bull for breeding, with three combines, two balers and eight tractors.

Also in the 1960s, Woodlands Poultry Farm, owned by Mr E.E. Calver, consisted of 12 acres; 8 acres of grassland, 4 acres for deep litter poultry houses breeding over 10, 000 cobb broiler breeders and producing over 7,000 eggs per day.

Also at this time, Mr L. Keech owned Peak Hill Farm in Milton Road, consisting of 5 acres, with over 4,000 battery hens and about 50 pigs.

5

The Boer War

Little is known about the Boer War of 1899 to 1902 in the history of Clapham, but it is recorded that there were eleven Clapham men serving in the Bedford Regiment in South Africa, in the Boer campaign.

It was during this time that the Curate of Clapham, the Reverend Vaughan-Evans, who lived in Bedford at the time, used to give lantern slide lectures about the war.

The lectures were held in the schoolroom and sometimes the room was so overcrowded that some villagers couldn't get in if they came a bit late. I can only assume why the room would get so crowded was because news at that time was scarce. People relied on newspaper reports for any information, which was much slower getting through than nowadays. The most famous war correspondent of the time was Winston Churchill.

~ 6 ~

Facts & Events In Clapham
1800 – late 1900s

Clapham, being just two miles away from Bedford, didn't just depend on agriculture, for there were other forms of employment. Many of the womenfolk went into service with the gentry, some in Clapham and others in Bedford. Many of my ancestors did this type of work, while the men went either into the building industry (my grandfather included) or engineering. Some were grocers or solicitors, in fact any form of employment that was available.

As mentioned in a previous chapter, in those early days of the twentieth century, Clapham had many local businesses of its own without going into Town. Transport wasn't prominent then, so people either had to walk, or go on their bicycle (if they owned one of course!), even by pony and trap, to get to work.

There was a carrier's cart that would take people, if there was room, but he would make a small charge for his services.

The first bus service to Clapham, wasn't until just before or in 1928. It ran from Bedford to the Fox and Hounds Public House. Franklin's was one of the first company buses about at that time.

It was about this time in the 1920s that the brickyards and kilns closed down. This was another employer for the area. The brickyard was along Clapham Road next to Franklin's cottages, to where the Anglian Waterworks are today. It had been in existence since about the early 1800s. The ground along there was hard, heavy clay. The bricks made there were mostly the blue engineering type, although they did make the ordinary common brick as well.

~ 1900 ~

The old Clapham Church of England School was found to be too small with 176 children on roll and so it was extended to include an infants' room, which cost £147. Miss Annie Elizabeth Williams was the Headmistress at this time. At the turn of the century many of the children at the school suffered with whooping-cough and ringworm. Just before the First World War, the local County Medical Officer would sometimes close the school because of an outbreak of mumps and measles.

During the first part of the twentieth century, the one big occasion for the village was the Clapham Feast. It was held in early July of each year and on this day of celebration, most of the relatives of the village people would come to Clapham to see their families. They didn't just come from Bedford, but from other villages around as well.

Some of the village people would have been busy for weeks, making and preparing food; nearly everyone made some sort of contribution. At one time it was held on the wide pathway where the entrance to Ursula Taylor

The old Ursula Taylor Primary School, built in 1872, demolished in the 1990s to make way for new housing.

The new Ursula Taylor Primary School, built in the 1970s.

School entrance is today. The long trestle tables came right out onto the road, all loaded with food of every description. Of course there wasn't the traffic about in those days, not like today, just the odd horse and cart, or a pony and trap, going up and down the High Street.

As the village increased in population, the Feast was held in fields next to the Clapham Clubhouse. There were no houses there then. In the years before the Second World War, there would be a small fair come to add a further attraction to the Feast Day. The whole village in those days would join in the fun of Clapham Feast - alas, nowadays, no longer celebrated.

In the so-called 'good old days' of years ago, and long before television and radio, the only entertainment people had, was what they put on themselves. That's how it was in Clapham in the early 1900s, when concerts were held in the schoolroom. As there was no other entertainment, the concerts used to get pretty crowded with the village people. I suppose at that time most were glad to get out of their, mostly, cramped, draughty houses. The concerts were mainly audience participation; some would sing, someone would give a dialogue, there was even a gramophone played, followed by fancy dancing at times. Everyone would join in the fun, young or old.

Some of the concerts put on were to raise money for the Rural District Nurses, and other good causes of that time.

When the Sunday School held their party and prize-giving ceremonies, they would be given a treat by being taken to the Woodlands Manor House, where some sort of entertainment was put on. Afterwards the children would then be presented with a large bag of sweets by the owner, Mr Fitzpatrick. It seems to me that there was more 'togetherness' by the people of the village than there is today, probably because Clapham was less populated than now.

It was in these years that the then Borough Councillor, Mr Arthur Black, along with the Parish Council, were looking at ways and means as to how land could be provided in Clapham, for the purpose of allotments.

~ 1906 ~

It was in 1906 that the Church had to have two of its bells re-cast. When they were re-hung, they added another bell to the Church at the same time.

~ 1910 ~

The Parish Council were concerned with the poor delivery of the mail in the village. They had discussed this and agreed to write to the Head Postmaster in Bedford, to ask if it was possible to have the post delivered three times a day.

The local farmers in 1910 were getting quite concerned about the bad weather as there had been so much rain. The gathering of the harvest had been considerably checked back because the fields were saturated with water. (Not a lot changes!)

It was during 1910 and 1911 that meetings were going on with the Bedford Borough Council and the Reverend Besket, who was the owner of The Brick and Tile Works near Cut-throat Lane. The Borough Council wanted to buy the old brickyards and use the land for The Bedford Water Company, and thought it was the best site for a waterworks. The meetings went on for some time because the Reverend Besket was asking too much money for the site, which was £10,000. After more meetings, the Borough Council decided that they would compulsorily purchase the Brickyards if no agreement could be met. In the end the Reverend Besket relented and accepted the sum of £ 8,000 for the site. With the brickyards sold to the Bedford Water Company, they cleared the site, and in later years built a waterworks.

1914 ~ 1918

There were quite a few of the young men of the village who were called up, to join the Army at the outbreak of World War I. A number of them didn't return. Their names are on a marble tablet on the north chancel in the Church, and on one of the pillars at the entrance to the Playing Field. Their names are:

A. Armstrong	S. Foster
A.G. Baker	A.T. Gilbert
C.A. Brown	J.W. Gudgeon
E.W. Barker	A.T. Jones
C.A. Bland	H.T. Pettit
C.H. Browning	G. Robinson
L. Bower	J.E. Shadbolt
C. Colbert	E. Single
R.D. Colbert	F.W. Smith
A. Craddock	G. Theobald
N.F. Devereux	D. Waller

During the First World War my grandfather, Frederick Kirby volunteered for the Army at the age of 49 years, as a recruiting sergeant. He was a tall, well built man, and with his puttees around the calves of his legs, he really looked the part. He not only went around Bedfordshire, but travelled around the country as well, recruiting men for the Army.

My father was also in the First World War. He was in the Army serving in the R.A.M.C. in the 10th Field

Ambulance Brigade. He did his service in France, where the Germans used mustard gas. My father suffered the rest of his life with a bad mouth as a consequence of the gas. (In 1926 he was one of the founder members of the Clapham branch of the British Legion, today known as the Royal British Legion. He was also the first Secretary of the Clapham Branch, and in 1930 was selected to go, with others from the Bedford Section, to France for a memorial reunion.)

With the First World War starting in 1914, there wasn't much activity in Clapham at this time, as most of the young men of the village were being called up or volunteering to fight. However, there was an incident recorded in the *Bedfordshire Times* of an Organ Grinder by the name of Tony Orpins, who apparently was making a nuisance of himself. One night he was stopped by the local Policeman for riding his Organ Grinder without any lights. That was a serious offence in those days. He was sent to Court, where he was fined 1s (or 5p) plus 1s 6d (7½p) in costs.

During the war years there were several 'magic lantern' lectures taking place in the Schoolroom about the war. One of these lectures was called "Fighting on Land, Sea and Air" and was given by Mr J.L. Fishwick. There were always large audiences in the Schoolroom to listen to them.

Towards the end of the war, several of the Clapham soldiers were allowed home on hospital leave, most were suffering from gas inhalation.

In the July of 1918, the Clapham District Nurse, Nurse Freeman, decided to retire. To mark her seventeen years' service to the village, a testimonial was arranged in the Schoolroom, where she was presented with a gold watch and £10.10s.

As the war came to a close, several of the ex-prisoners who came from Clapham and other villages and towns around Bedfordshire, attended a reception at the Corn Exchange in Bedford. It was given to celebrate their homecoming.

~ 1919 ~

In the new year of 1919, several villagers complained that the church bells were not rung at Christmas time and the New Year. The Vicar explained that it was because some of the bell boys had been prisoners of war, and he wanted them to settle back. He promised that the bells would ring in celebration of their return.

~ 1920 ~

It wasn't until the early part of the 1920s that Clapham had the mains services laid on. The village during this time was being dug up, time and time again. This was to allow the mains water, gas, and electricity to be connected to the village. It was all done by hand by the navvies - no mechanical diggers in those days! – Even when they had finished there were still several houses without these facilities. At this time Clapham had more fields than houses, from Highbury Grove right up to Milton Road, there were very few houses on either side of the road.

Each year during the 1920s the Church would hold a concert and a party for the villagers, which was held in the Chapel schoolroom. Also around the same time the Church Choir held their annual supper, in which the vicar, the Reverend J.K. Cowburn, would thank them for their services in the past year. My mother was a member of the choir during this time.

~ 1921 ~

It was in 1921 that Mr Harold Rush, the Farmer at Church Farm, was killed in his two-seater motor car. He was burnt to death on Brogborough Hill when his car burst into flames. His wife, Mary, carried on at the farm for a while.

~ 1926 ~

In the late 1920s and early 1930s there was the Depression throughout the country and in 1926 was the General Strike. Many people were without work, including many in Clapham. It was an awful time for many people.

~ 1927/28 ~

The winter of 1927 and 1928 was a traumatic one for many of the people who lived in the High Street at that time. In the January of 1928, after a heavy fall of snow and then rain, a thaw set in and swelled the river and streams with melting snow. This caused one of the worst floods Clapham had known in living memory. Many of the houses, if not all, in the High Street, were flooded out downstairs. The main road was flooded from the Chapel to the Folly for a couple of days. By the third day the water had swelled even more, bringing lots of debris down the High Street. The swollen water made its way even further down the High Street until it had reached the Ford. With the houses having two or three feet of water in them, people just took as much as they could upstairs, where they had to stay for a day or two. The only way people could get any food was when the baker came up the village street by boat and delivered bread on the end of a long stick. All transport, such as buses and cars, had to turn back. Nothing could get through. A horseman by the name of Mr E. Newell, an ex-postmaster of Oakley, tried to ride his horse through the flood, but the water came up to the horse's chest so he decided to turn back.

After the floods had receded came the gales, causing widespread damage throughout the village. It must have been a distressing and stressful time for the people.

Because of the floods and gales which followed, the Women's Institute held their meeting a week late, in the Reading Room in the Warren. A competition was held for the best packed dinner for a man at work, and had to cost no more than 9d (4p). I wonder if that's how we got to the packed lunches of today?

In the last few days of January 1928, a Mr Fred Dunham, who worked on the London Midland and Scottish Railway as a wireman, fell down an embankment and broke his leg. He was taken to the Bedford Hospital, where he was made comfortable. On the same day, a Miss Lilly Taylor, aged just four years old, was knocked down by a car in the High Street, but fortunately was not seriously hurt. Luckily Nurse Wilson, the local District Nurse, was on hand to attend to her.

In the December of 1928, the Horse and Groom Savings Club, under the chairmanship of Mr Frank Pickering (my father), had their annual share-out and held a Christmas Dinner in the public house.

~ 1929 ~

At the Clapham and Oakley Nursing Association Meeting, it was reported that Nurse Eva Wilson had had a very busy year. She had attended 11 births, 87 surgical cases and 174 medical cases altogether, making over 1,000 visits. She was Clapham's best known and popular District Nurse and Midwife who delivered both myself and my wife. She lived in the High Street opposite The Warren. You would often see her around at all hours in her matron style uniform, either walking or riding her bicycle. Nurse Wilson was a great character of the village and died sometime in the 1950s.

Poultry farmers in 1929 were complaining about foxes. Apparently they had been on the rampage, killing several chickens, also taking them from their coops. Nothing changes for the poor old fox. It is still hounded to this day.

At the side of The Ford, and next to where the old thatched Tollgate Cottage stood at this time, stood a large wooden building. John Howard of Clapham Park had it built on land owned by Charles Wells of the Bedford Brewery Co., who charged a small rent. It was erected for John Howard's daughters, Kathleen and Audrey. It was Audrey who ran the Girl Guides. The W.I. held their meetings there also. Kathleen was President of the Clapham W.I., Audrey was the Treasurer. At one time Kathleen was the W.I. County Chairman and later the County President. She died in 1980 aged 90 years. In later years the building became the Parish Hall.

It shows you the difference in the changing times, for it was in the February of 1929 that a carpenter who worked for a Bedford Builder, was working on a site in Felmersham. He knew the job would take at least three days to do, but after the first day, his boss told him to stay later and finish the job, which he did. He knew that as it was dark, and he had no lights on his bike, he would have to ride carefully without being caught. He left Felmersham with his tool kit on his handlebars, but when he reached Clapham, he was stopped by the local policeman. The carpenter was subsequently taken to court, where he was fined five shillings (25p) for riding his bicycle without any lights. In today's world I suppose he would claim compensation from his boss.

~ 1930 ~

By 1930 a fund was opened for the overhauling of the Canon Haddock Memorial Clock as the old school clock was found to be in a bad state.

~ 1931 ~

By 1931 the population of the village was 811. It hadn't grown much in thirty years.

~ 1934 ~

Part of Clapham was transferred to the Bedford Borough Council in 1934, but most of the village still came under the Rural District Council.

By 1934, Clapham began to grow in size, for at this time there were several pairs of houses being built, not only in the High Street, but in other areas around Clapham as well. This was the time that Mr F.P. Tinsley, the local builder, began to develop a new street in the middle of the village. As the houses began to take shape, he was going to call the new Street Thrift Street, but the people of the village rebelled against such a name. After a meeting, the villagers won their day, for they were able to persuade Mr Tinsley to change his mind. He then decided to call the street Highbury Grove, which met with unanimous approval. The people rebelled because at that time, they couldn't afford to be anything but thrifty because it wasn't long after the Depression, and money was tight. So there is nothing new in 'people power', as some people think today, it was around Clapham in the 1930s.

Highbury Grove at that time had several cherry trees along both sides of it. The cherries were inedible and made a mess as they fell off. The trees on the right hand side of the road were taken down when the bungalows were built on the field known as 'The Rec', but the others remained until about 1960 when they were either vandalised or taken down because of their age. There is just one tree left today.

Highbury Grove in the 1930s, before the new bungalows were built on the 'Rec'.

1939 ~ 1945

By 1939 the Second World War was looming, and again there was a lot of uncertainty. In the September of that year war had started. Once again families had their husbands, sons and daughters called up to join the services.

It was in the May of 1939 that the Clapham W.V.S. was formed by Mrs A.C. Farr, and it wasn't long before 26 members had enrolled. It was formed for the readiness of war, which was expected at any time. They had basic training lectures on First Aid, and in water supply from the various water wells around the village, and in billeting accommodation ready for the evacuees that were expected. They also made camouflage net tops for tin hats, mostly for the local Home Guard. The W.V.S. took an active part in the Salvage Campaign, going around the village with a horse and cart, collecting aluminium, rags, and other useful objects that could be used for the war effort. The Clapham W.V.S. worked hard raising funds by various means, for the Village Comfort Fund for Soldiers throughout the war years.

The Clapham Women's Institute also had a programme of 'special weeks', raising funds for what was known as 'The Spitfire Fund', 'Salute to the Soldier', and for war weapons. The village ladies certainly played their part in raising funds for the war effort.

Air Raid Warden activities were also going on, with Mr E.H. Dixon in charge. They used the Church, Chapel and later, Clapham Club as the meeting points. Luckily they were not in action much as no bombs fell on the village. The only incident attended was a crashed training plane which burst into flames, killing the two airmen. The incident happened at the Folly end of the village in Milton Road.

Throughout the war years Clapham Farms kept going. They had at least six land-girls working on the land, who all proved to be most satisfactory. There were also ten German and two Italian POWs working on the farms around. Although the labour problems were difficult, there was 75% more food produced in Clapham than the previous five years before 1939. It was a marvellous achievement.

In Clapham, like many other villages throughout the Country in 1940, the Home Guard began, or 'Dad's Army' as it would be known today. Clapham had quit a large contingency of not only older men, but young men as well in the Home Guard. Their Headquarters was at the Clapham Club, where the War Ministry compulsorily took over a room. They sealed the inner door and had a purpose-built entrance door put in from the outside. Inside the room was a bed, which was used for the night-time firewatchers, there was also a gun safe. As the war intensified, a lot of the young men were called up into the Services. My elder brother Reg was one of them. He went into the RAF for the rest of the war.

Reuben Albert Vincent Wright (Bert) as he was known, who would have been my father-in-law had he lived, served in the Bedfordshire Territorial Army in the late 1930s. When war came he went into the 5th Beds & Herts Regiment. In 1942 he sailed with his comrades to Singapore. After they had landed, the Regiment was captured by the Japanese. He endured unbelievably bad treatment, like the rest of them in Changi camp, until his death in May 1945. My wife never really knew her father; she was only two years old when he went away.

Things in Britain dramatically changed in 1942 for the Americans had now entered the war and many of them were stationed around the country, including Bedfordshire. Among them was the American 8th Airforce Service Command. Some of them, mostly officers, were billeted at Milton Ernest Hall, but most of the servicemen were at Thurleigh, Twinwoods, Risely and Little Staughton, also other airfields around.

I remember when as a small boy, seeing their large camouflaged army trucks going backwards and forwards through Clapham. Somehow I always felt safe when I heard them rumbling back from a night out in Bedford.

In those days there was an American Red Cross and GI Club in the town which stood on the corner of Union Street with Bromham Road.

Twinwoods was known as the Beaufighter Base, although there were also five squadrons of R.A.F. Mustangs stationed there. In those early years of the war, Beaufighters and Mosquitos flew from some of the airfields, but when the Americans arrived, it was the famous B29s or Flying Fortress that were seen in the skies over Clapham. They were a marvellous aircraft, their engines having a familiar drone to them. You really felt safe when they went over! When you were a ten-year-old boy, as I was, you didn't realize that some of those aeroplanes, and the brave young fighters in them, would not be making it back.

By the summer of 1944, the American band leader, Major Glenn Miller, had arrived in Britain. The band gave several concerts and held dances at various venues, as well as making many recordings in London at the Abbey Road studios. After a while, the band, now known as The American Band of the Supreme Allied Command, decided to leave London which was now a very dangerous place because of the heavy bombing and the flying bombs. Major Glenn Miller and the band came to Bedford. The band stayed at Co-Partners Hall in Queens Park, but Glenn Miller stayed at Milton Ernest Hall. The Americans, or GIs as they were known, soon made friends, especially with the girls from the villages. Some even eventually married.

Glenn Miller was only in Britain for just six months, but during that time he had made a huge impact on the town of Bedford. On a glorious day in the July of 1944, Glenn Miller and the American Band of the Supreme Allied Command gave their first airfield concert at Thurleigh airfield. It included a string section and was now a forty piece orchestra. Two days later, the full Orchestra and Strings, performed in the grounds of Milton Ernest Hall. The following weeks the Orchestra would perform at other bases around the Country, including Northern Ireland. All the venues were always well attended by the servicemen and women, either sitting or standing, and applauding the marvellous sound coming from the Orchestra.

Little did I realise who it was at the time, but I was told that it was the great bandleader himself that I saw opposite my house one day, as his jeep had broken down and was being attended to at Henman's Garage.

Glenn Miller and the Orchestra gave many concerts and dances for the servicemen at the Corn Exchange. They also made many recordings, making eighty-eight programmes in eighteen days at one time. The Orchestra did most of their rehearsals at the Co-Partners Hall in Queens Park.

They were not the only orchestra to rehearse there, for also in Bedford at this time was the BBC Symphony Orchestra and their conductor, Sir Adrian Boult. They also had fled London because of the bombing. The Symphony Orchestra also gave many concerts at the Corn Exchange and made many recordings. Sir Adrian Boult was living at Woodlands Manor House in Clapham throughout this time.

In the December of 1944, the Allies thought it would boost the morale of the troops if the Orchestra went to Europe. It was all part of the propaganda campaign. It was arranged that the Orchestra went on to Paris, while Glenn Miller was to follow the next day.

After lunch on a very foggy day of 15th December 1944, Major Glenn Miller boarded a single engined

Norseman UC64a, and took off from Twinwoods. He was never seen again. The concert did go ahead in Paris, but in a very subdued atmosphere.

A lot has been said and written about the disappearance of Glenn Miller, whether true or false we shall never know. I only know that he gave a lot of pleasure all over the world with his wonderful music, and still does to this day, through records, tapes and CDs.

The control tower at Twinwoods (below), where Glenn Miller spent his final hours in Britain, is still standing to this day, if a little dilapidated. It has an eerie presence about it.

In 1944 there were 100 Clapham men, all ranks, serving in the Army. There were 20 in the Navy and 24 in the RAF. Of the girls serving from the village there were four in the ATS, four in the WAAF and two in the WRNS. There were 14 men who were prisoners of war or missing, and by 1944, seven village men had lost their lives fighting for their country.

It was during the 1940s that there were 208 evacuees in Clapham. Most came from the London area. It was noted that some were of good type, some were rough types and dirty, all various kinds. Some stayed throughout the war, and after.

During the 1940s, the Manor House in Clapham Park, owned by John Howard, was requisitioned by the Ministry of Supply. It was used for a rehabilitation centre for the Forces. In 1948 The Manor Hospital acquired the place. Also at the same time, the Woodlands Manor was requisitioned by the Ministry of Supply, and used for emergency accidents which occurred during the blackout. It was manned around the clock. Woodlands was sold to the Ministry of Supply in 1951.

~ 7 ~

Clapham's King George V Playing Field

Where I lived in the High Street, at the back of our house was an agricultural field. Wheat, barley, maize and carrots were grown in it.

I remember one glorious summer's day during the wartime. I was in the field with my mother, and we were gleaning. Also in the field were some German prisoners of war who were working away picking up the sheaves left by the binder, and putting them into shocks. They didn't take any notice of my mother and I as we picked up the odd corn ears and put them in the sack. In those days we kept a lot of chickens at the bottom of our long garden, so we used to go gleaning to help with the feed, also pick up some of the hay for bedding. In those days there was no combine harvester, so all the corn was cut by the reaper.

After the harvest had been gathered in, the field was left fallow for a while, then it was time for ploughing. I had many a ride on the Caterpillar tractor as it went up and down ploughing the field. At that time you could look out of the back windows of our house and see the fields stretch right up to Twinwoods. The last crop that was grown in the field was maize.

Way back in 1936, the Lord Mayor of London's National Memorial Fund Committee made an appeal to the Nation for funds for a statue in London in remembrance of King George V, and for playing fields throughout the country. In 1939 the forward thinking Clapham Parish Council of the time applied for, and accepted a grant of £1,000. Unfortunately the war delayed their plans and by 1944, the cost had risen to £4,321, of which £1,334 was for the cost of the land, which the Parish Council purchased from the Ministry of Health. A lot of the money was raised by the Playing Field Fund Committee who held various functions in

CLAPHAM
KING GEORGE'S FIELD

Official

Opening

SOUVENIR PROGRAMME
6d.

23rd April, 1949

2.30 p.m.   The proceedings will commence with a Dedication Service by the British Legion and the unveiling of the War Memorial Panels, followed by the official opening of the field by Lord Luke.

3 p.m.   The Football and Netball Teams will be presented to Lord Luke, who has kindly consented to start each game.

FOOTBALL MATCH

| CLAPHAM F.C. v. LYNTON WORKS F.C. ♭

Clapham

S. BLUNT

D. CRANE   T. BUCK

R. LETT   G. FARRER   G. OAKINS

R. DEVEREUX   E. SUMMERFIELD   A. DEVEREUX   R. NORTON   R. SANDERS

Referee: MR. F. KNIGHT

Linesmen: MR. R. FACEY, MR. E. PESTEL

CAVES   CLARIDGE   HARPER   LEE   SCOTT

TICEHURST   BEARDSMORE   HARVEY

BEARDSMORE   GRAY

ARMSTRONG

Lynton Works

FOOTBALL MATCH

| CLAPHAM SCHOOL v. SHARNBROOK SCHOOL |

Clapham School

J. BAKER

G. WATLING   B. HUNT

R. HENMAN   G. BODSWORTH   R. MADDAMS

A. KING   T. PRIOR   J. PICKERING   G. NORMAN   M. PASS

Referee: MR. D. WILLIAMS

Linesmen: D. GOODWIN, G. DEAS

M. STRINGER   J. BOYLES   J. MACKENZIE   G. HOLYOAK   R. PURSER

R. RICHARDSON   H. PAULL   J. SHAYLER

J. HULLATT   O. DICKERSON

D. BAYES

Sharnbrook School

NETBALL MATCH

SCHOOL v. THE REST

(*The Rest is a team of Clapham girls attending other Schools*)

Umpires: MR. E. WILKINSON and MR. R. R. BAMBER

	School	The Rest
Goal Keeper	D. ROGERS	H. BUCK
Defence	V. ROGERS	P. WILKINSON
Defending Centre	B. LINCOLN	A. GROSE
Centre	S. ROBERTS	P. SWALES
Attacking Centre	H. KEECH	A. ASTBURY
Attack	B. HAYWARD	P. MUGGLETON
Shooter	A. PEACOCK	Y. HALES

Tea will be provided by the Clapham Sports and Social Club
at the Parish Hall for Guests and Players taking part

8 p.m. DANCE (Modern and Old-Time Dances) in THE HALL
ADMISSION 1s. 6d. *Proceeds in aid of the Playing Field.*

CAR PARK: Highbury Grove (by kind permission of Mr. F. P. Tinsley)

OFFICIAL OPENING
AND
UNVEILING OF TWO WORLD WAR
MEMORIAL PANELS

at 2.30 P.M., by

The Rt. Hon. LORD LUKE, D.L., J.P.

Deputy Chairman National Playing Fields Association
Chairman Silver Jubilee Appeal Committee
Chairman Beds. Playing Fields Association

SUPPORTED BY OFFICERS AND MEMBERS OF
THE BEDFORDSHIRE PLAYING FIELDS ASSOCIATION

Foreword

By FRANCIS L. WELCH

(Honorary Secretary Bedfordshire Playing Fields Association)

It was a rare inspiration which led the British people to adopt Playing Fields as their Memorial to a gracious and well beloved King. Nothing would have given greater pleasure to His late Majesty than to see the well designed and admirally equipped Playing Fields which bear his name in many parts of the country.

Clapham is an excellent example of these and reflects the greatest credit on the Parish Council and all others associated in this enterprise.

I only hope that this splendid lead will be followed by many other villages in Bedfordshire where Playing Fields are urgently needed if the young people are to enjoy the health giving recreation in the open air which is their natural birthright.

KING GEORGE'S FIELDS

In 1936, the Lord Mayor of London's National Memorial Fund Committee made its appeal to the nation for funds for a statue in London and Playing Fields throughout the country.

The unveiling by His Majesty the King of the Statue of King George V in 1947 forms part of the National Memorial to this greatly beloved monarch. An essential part of the scheme is the "King George's Fields" (Clapham being one of over 500) which bear on their gates the heraldic panels which are the distinguishing mark of all fields prepared under this Scheme.

Clapham made application for a grant in March 1939 and accepted in May of that year the offer of £1,000 and the conditions of the King George's Field Foundation. The outbreak of war considerably delayed the carrying out of the scheme which was eventually begun late in 1944. The approved capital cost of the Scheme in 1939 was £2,555 but already in an uncompleted state it has cost £4,321; £1,334 *of this being the cost of the land* which the Parish Council obtained permission from the Ministry of Health to transfer to the use of the Playing Field. The cost has been met by an increased foundation grant of £1,500, £1,304 raised by the Playing Field Committees, the £1,334, *value of the land, transferred by the Parish Council,* and the balance, over a number of years, from the rates.

Provision is now made for a Children's Corner with equipment, one Senior Football Pitch, one Junior Football Pitch, one Hockey Pitch, one Cricket Table, a Sports Pavilion and a tool shed.

FUTURE DEVELOPMENTS. It is hoped to add four tennis courts, a bowling green (six rinks) and a village hall, install electric light, construct a roadway and footpaths.

The only way in which this can be achieved is through the energetic efforts of Committees with the backing and co-operation of the whole village.

the village, with the balance coming from the rates. Clapham has a lot to thank the Parish Council of the day for, for having the foresight of wanting a playing field for the village in those prewar days.

During 1946 we watched the field transform into the Playing Field. The work was carried out by R. Quemby & Sons, who at that time, were farmers up at Twinwoods. The first year the field was too stony for games, and had to be de-stoned and re-seeded.

During 1947 the large cricket square was laid down. Most of the work was carried out by the Cricket Club members. I remember all the hard work that players of the day put into it to make it a lovely playing surface. Now today it is rarely played on. Water was also piped up to the square so that the pitch could be well watered. The water tap is still there to this day.

The Cricket Club had some marvellous games in the Playing Field, and went on to win most of the Beds. Cricket Leagues, including the Premier League in 1964. Not long after, the Cricket Club folded through lack of players.

The first football match in the field was against Harrold Reserves, with the Clapham vicar, the Reverend Cowburn, starting the match by kicking off.

The Playing Field was officially opened on the 23rd of April 1949 by the Rt. Hon. Lord Luke of Pavenham, supported by officers and members of the Bedfordshire Playing Fields Association. A large crowd gathered to hear his opening speech which was followed by a short dedication service by the British Legion, and the unveiling of the war memorial panels on the pillars of the entrance gates. The names of the Clapham men who died in the Second World War are:

J. BIRBECK	W. McKENNAN
K. DENNIS	C. PRIOR
S. FOX	J. SPRIGGS
J. HULME	H. SUMMERS
N. LOAK	J.L. WHITE
W. MILLER	R. WRIGHT

After the dedication service two football matches took place.

There was also a girls' netball match between the Clapham schoolgirls and the rest made up of Clapham girls who attended other schools. Clapham football team played a team from the Lynton Works. Clapham lost 6-1, while the Clapham schoolboys played Sharnbrook schoolboys and drew 1-1. Both games were played in

Clapham's King George V Playing Field

good spirit, and everyone enjoyed them. (The football team went on to win most of the Beds. Football Leagues, also the Britannia Cup over the years).

Afterwards, tea was provided by the Clapham Sports and Social Club at the Parish Hall, for guests and players taking part. Later a dance was held in the Parish Hall, with both modern and old time dancing to records. It ended a marvellous day for the people of Clapham.

In the children's area at that time there was a tall slide, an American swing, a roundabout, several large swings and a few baby swings as well. They were all well used in those days, never any vandalism anyway. There was also a split shelter so that mothers could keep an eye on their children, while on the other side people could watch the various games being played. At one time there was a tarmac surface tennis court in the field.

In the 1950s the Annual Fete was held in the field, and one year even a Gymkhana, but it was the only one as I suppose the horses cut up the field too much.

The Sports and Social Club in the 1950s contributed a Bingo stall, which was made and run by

Mr Ron Farrar and Mr Cliff Inskip, with Mr Alf Evans doing the electrics on it. It was a marvellous stall and they also took it around to other fetes and shows in Bedfordshire. All the money raised went into the Playing Field Fund for sports equipment and other amenities.

The bye-laws of the playing field were drawn up by the Parish Council, and were approved by the seal of the Secretary of State at the Home Office by Mr J. Chuter-Ede in 1951. The Labour Party were in Government at this time.

One of the by-laws states:

'A *person shall not deface or injure or destroy any wall, fence, any building, barrier, railing, post or seat, or any erection or ornament in the ground.' It goes on to say that 'Any person who shall offend against any of the bye-laws shall be convicted to a fine of £2.'*

So vandals should beware!

In the early days of the playing field, the Cricket Club had a small wooden hut which stood at the top end of the field. It was used for the scorers, storage for the gear and changing room. At the back was an enclosed area where the nets and goalposts were stored for the football team.

In those early days the toilet facilities were very poor, for they were just the portable type inside an old corrugated iron shack affair – not very nice at all. After a while the Parish Council had some dressing rooms built, which included toilet facilities and showers. The building is still there today but the toilets had to be bricked up because of vandalism. An enclosed area was added later for storage of the goalposts, nets, etc., also the large roller used for the cricket pitch.

In the first years several poplar trees were planted on the allotments side, and have matured well. In recent years more trees have been planted around the field, and it is nice to see them maturing, despite the efforts of the vandals trying to destroy them. To me, the trees can only enhance the playing field, for they are not just a thing of beauty, but will give shade as well over the years. With the seats that are all around, it can be a quiet place to sit or watch children at play. The playing field is a great asset to the village, and I am sure it is the envy of many villages around.

In the 1960s, the Community Centre was built in the playing fields grounds. The old wooden building by the Ford, built in 1929, was beginning to come to the end of its usefulness and needed a lot of repairs to it. It had been badly burnt in the 1950s. It was used five days a week for the school dinners and one of the ovens started the fire.

8

Clapham Club

In the early 1800s, James Howard, the founder of Clapham Working Men's Club as it was known then, decided to form a committee to run the Club. It was during those early years that the Club just sold tea and coffee, also oil and coal, but no alcohol. James Howard didn't approve of alcoholic beverages. The Club also had a library, all the books being donated by the president and the committee.

The first secretary of the Club was Mr Frederick Tinsley, a local farmer. The membership at this time was a total of sixty-five male members.

The only lighting for the Club at this time was from oil lamps, and the heating was from coal fires. Indeed, coal fires were the only heating up to the late 1950s. As for the toilet facilities, they were abysmal, for they were the old cesspool type. The main services didn't reach Clapham until the 1920s. I suppose the river running behind the Club came in handy at times!

After a few years the committee wanted to sell beer, wine and spirits but as James Howard was so much against this, he decided to sell the Club.

The committee were so adamant, they turned to the Higgins Brewery in Bedford, from whom they borrowed money. Once this was done the Club began to thrive.

By 1887 the Club was financially sound, even having money in the bank to the sum of £21.2s.8d (£21.13). The price of a pint of beer at this time was 2d (1½p) a pint. A tot of rum was 3d (1½p). You could even get a pint of whisky which was served up in a stone jar for 3/- (15p).

The membership also increased considerably, averaging thirty-four members attending daily throughout the year.

Entertainment in those early days was made by the members themselves. Someone would play a mouth-organ or a concertina, then someone would sing a song or two. Once a year the Bromham bell-ringers would come to the Club and give a concert.

The Club went from strength to strength and in 1921 the Committee bought a snooker table – the same table is used to this day by the members. The Club also had a quoits pitch on the lawn at the back of the Club.

In 1941 the War Ministry commandeered the games room which was used for the local Home Guard (Dad's Army) Headquarters. Three beds were put inside the room for the fire-watchers and guard patrol at night. It was restored back to the Club in 1944.

The Club has gone on to be a successful Club, with membership rising at one time to over a thousand in the 1960s and 1970s. Known nowadays as just Clapham Club, it is still a thriving Club.

The Clapham Branch of the Royal British Legion hold their monthly meetings there and their annual buffet party. The Committee also let out the lounge for parties, which helps to bring in more revenue for the Club.

The original Henman's Garage in 1927.

*A car belonging to the Henmans in the 1920s
(note the petrol can on the running board).*

9

Henman's Garage
A Clapham Family Business

It was in the 1920s that George Henman, who was a cabinet maker for Wells, the Bedford furniture company, became fascinated with motorbikes. He used to tinker around with them, taking them apart, then putting them back together again. His passion for motorbikes was so strong that he decided to give up his job and work with motorbikes full time.

His son, Harold, who had been a dispatch rider in the Royal Flying Corps (later to become the RAF) in the 1914-18 War, was also fascinated with motorbikes.

George Henman bought a large wooden building in Clapham in 1925, and with his son, Harold, started the Henman Garage. At first it was motorbikes and cycles that they repaired and sold as well.

By 1927 they had acquired a tall petrol pump which was worked by hand, pumping up and down. In those days petrol was sold in cans, and most cars of the day had running boards to which the motorists would strap two or three cans of petrol. I don't think they thought of the safety aspect at the time.

By 1929 the Clapham Garage as it came to be known, was well established. Unfortunately the garage didn't generate enough income for both George and Harold to live on and Harold had a young family to support.

As Harold was an accomplished pianist, in 1930 he formed a dance band. It was known as 'The Blue Rhythm Band'. With Harold as its leader, they soon became very successful. They played at most of the ballrooms around Bedfordshire, and did so up to the war years.

In 1942 George Henman died, so it was left to Harold to carry on with the business. The garage was now called H.G. Henman & Son.

It was during the war years that Harold had a large black Vauxhall limousine, a seven-seater, which had a large glass panel to separate the passengers from the driver. It was a really beautiful car which he used as a taxi. I think at that time it was the only taxi service in Clapham. It was stored for a few years before it was sold.

Throughout the war years, Harold was a Special Police Constable, and worked alongside the village policeman, who at that time was P.C. Dennis.

In the 1950s Henmans had an expansion programme, with the garage going completely over to motor car repairs and sales. It was during this time in the 1950s that Harold Henman had his old cottage, which had stood at the side of the garage, demolished. He had built a large house with an office attached.

After Harold died in 1967 at the age of 64 years, his wife, along with her four sons, Ray, Alan, Ron and Colin, who were all on the Board of Directors of the Garage now, with Ray taking overall charge, carried on with Harold's devotion to the motor car business.

In the 1970s Henmans became the main dealers for the Reliant car, and they soon established the popularity of the Reliant Robin and the Kitten, not only in

Clapham but in other areas as well. With their servicing and after sales service, along with petrol sales, the business soon built up a solid reputation.

In the 1980s another extension to the garage took place. It was while the renovations were taking place that it was found that the old 500 gallon tank that had been underground since the 1920s was still in an immaculate condition as it was hauled out of the ground. With new modern equipment, service bays, along with the large car washing facilities, also the Q8 petrol sales, Henmans have established a high standard of proficiency. It was not surprising then, that the Government gave the official approval of a M.O.T. Certificate and a M.O.T. Licence for both three and four wheeled cars.

The Garage has been going now for over 80 years, and under the guidance of Harold Henman's youngest son, Colin, I'm sure it will go on for many more, for the Henman family have brought the real family traditions to the motor trade.

10

Two Clapham Mysteries

In 1853 a lead coffin was discovered in fields near to Milton Hill, but was found to be empty. Not far away from the coffin, several human remains were found. The theory is that they were probably troops, or an early Saxon burial place. Who was buried in the lead coffin? Was it someone of importance which was usually the case with a lead coffin, and whose were the human remains? Lots of questions, with no answers.

Another mystery of Clapham is how the top end of the village became to be known as 'the Folly'. A folly is usually thought to be a useless building of some kind.

Many years ago there was a clump of fir trees on the crest of a hill, near to where the 'Fox & Hounds' public house stands. Could it have been a copse or a spinney? Did they perhaps pull the trees down to make way for the building of the first 'Fox & Hounds' public house? It was built on land near to where the Oakley Hunt used to ride, so perhaps the old pub was known as the folly? Who knows.

Some say it was an odd piece of land jutting out at the side of the river. The site of this unusual shape could at one time be seen at the back of the Folly Caravan Park. Unfortunately most of that land has been eroded away over the years because of flooding. The mystery of Clapham Folly goes on - unless anyone knows different?

11

The Growth of Clapham from the 1950s

In 1946 the M.O.D. started an establishment for aerodynamic research and construction at Twinwoods and Thurleigh. It was to be known as the Royal Aircraft Establishment (RAE).

By 1948 they had constructed an access road which was off Milton Road behind Clapham Hospital. At the same time and into the early 1950s the M.O.D. started to have houses built at the top of Highbury Grove. They also established the roads of Cody Road and Lanchester Close at this time.

On the corner of Cody Road stood a single storey building which was the site office and building compound. Later it became a baby clinic, not only for the RAE but also for the young mothers of the village.

Twenty-five garages were built at the bottom of Lanchester Close with entrances into Cody Road and Highbury Grove. There were also two water taps, providing washing facilities for cars. It was on this site that a tragedy occurred on the 14th February 1978. The local press headed the story 'The St. Valentine's Day Massacre'.

Four maintenance men who worked for Barratts Developments Group had their shed in the corner of the garages. One of the workers' cars would not start on that fateful morning and he was late for work. When he did arrive and entered the workmen's shed, he was confronted by what must have been an appalling sight for he found three of his workmates lying dead – one had a shotgun by his side. All the men were middle aged. The incident happened at 8 a.m. that morning. It was thought that after an argument, one man shot two of his workmates and then turned the gun on himself. The dead men were Albert Hullat, a bricklayer, Thomas Miles, also a bricklayer, and Christopher Surridge, a carpenter.

It was in the late 1950s and early 1960s that the RAE had a club built from a converted store, which stood at the bottom of the access road, known today as Twinwoods Road. The Club, which is run by a committee, has seen many changes and improvements over the years. Today it is known as the DERA Club, and is still thriving as a family social club.

After about forty years, in the 1990s, the M.O.D. began to phase down and just left the wind tunnel site. Also at this time it was known as DERA (Defence Evaluation Research Agency Association). Most of the houses in Highbury Grove, Cody Road and Lanchester Close were sold off at this time.

In the mid 1950s, bungalows were erected up Highbury Grove, also on the old field known as the rec. There were more bungalows built further up, on the site of an old gravel pit. The roads of The Close and The Slade were made up at this time.

It was on the site of the gravel pit that one firework night in the early 1950s, a young soldier home on leave, was blown up by a grenade he had brought home.

More building work went on in the 1950s, this time a number of houses - were erected in Mount Pleasant Road, also on the surrounding fields. There were quite a few houses that were built, forming the roads of Knights Avenue, Queens Crescent and Dukes Drive. Clapham at this time was a growing village, with the population quickly increasing.

Even into the 1960s house building became prominent, with new houses being built up the top end of Highbury Grove, joining onto Knights Avenue. Also at the top of the Allotments more houses were built, forming the road of Bents Close.

It was at this time in 1962 that the old post-war prefabs in Princess Street had become a little dilapidated by now. The Council decided to pull them down, replacing them with two blocks of flats in Bents Close, (although one block fronts Highbury Grove), and the ex-prefabs residents moved into them. On the site of the prefabs two blocks of flats were erected to house Council house tenants and later transferred to Pilgrim Housing.

By the late 1960s/early 1970s bungalows were built on an old pre-war gravel pit and fields behind Mount Pleasant Road to form the new George Street.

Houses were being built at the side of the access road to the Royal Aircraft Establishment, also a few bungalows as well. This is when the roads of Bridle Drive, Saddle Close, Fetlock Close, and Paddock Close were all laid down. At the same time the Texaco Garage was erected.

In the late 1970s/early 1980s houses were built at the side of the old Clapham Hospital, to form Tinsley Close.

As more and more house building went on in Clapham, the main High Street began to have an explosion of traffic up and down it.

We entered the 1990s with more houses of the superior type being built in the old Clapham Park, also down The Baulk.

As we enter the new Millennium, the old Park Farm buildings have been converted into housing.

We now reach the Spring of 2001 and site clearance has begun along Milton Road, opposite Twinwoods

Road, the old R.A.E. access road, for the building of 2-300 hundred houses.

Work has begun on the RAE site, soon to become an immigration reception centre.

Clapham – A Summary

As we travel in time across two centuries to the present day we might well ask ourselves – What was Clapham? – What is Clapham? and What will Clapham become?

Clapham is seriously lacking in really old buildings. The oldest building still standing is the Church of St. Thomas á Becket of course, and even that went through some changes in earlier times, especially by the Saxons and Normans.

The old manor house that stood next to the church was pulled down in 1831, replaced by Church Farm House.

One of the oldest buildings still standing is the farm house at Park Farm, which dates back to the sixteenth/ seventeenth century. Others are the Woodlands Manor, built in 1812. The old manor house in Clapham Park, which James Howard had built in 1872 still stands in the grounds, but today it has been converted to luxury flats.

The chapel was built in 1876, the original chapel stood just inside the Warren and was built in 1829, but it fell into a state of disrepair. The new chapel was built just in time.

The Reading Room at the top of the Warren still stands, but looks a sorry sight and is no longer used. It was built between 1898 and 1900 on land sold for building in 1898. If Jesse Katharine Haddock were to return now, she might well be upset at seeing the building, which she bequeathed to the village in 1917, looking so forlorn.

Probably the oldest public house in the village is the Horse and Groom. No-one knows when it was first built, not even the Brewery Archives, as all the deeds have been lost. It was first licensed in 1705, but it was then known as 'The Horse and Jockey'. It changed its name to 'The Horse and Groom' in 1874.

'The Swan' was first licensed in 1873, and 'The Star' in 1896. Here again, the Charles Wells Archives can only

The Horse and Groom public house.

The Swan public house.

tell us when they were first licensed, and not when they were built, as all the deeds are lost.

'The Fox and Hounds' was once thatched, and re-built in its present form in 1926. From about 1846 it had been an ale house. It was first licensed in the 1870s.

Clapham Club was built by James Howard in 1879 as a social club selling tea and coffee, and a library of books contributed by the committee. James Howard sold the Club to the committee when they wanted to sell beer as he was dead against this. It then became Clapham Working Men's Club. In these politically correct times of gender equality, the Club is also for women members and so renamed simply as 'Clapham Club'.

Opposite The Warren there used to be a public house called 'The Vicar of Wakefield'. I have never known how it got that name. It was built sometime in the nineteenth century and started life as an ale house. It later became a public house and was first licensed in 1868. In the 1980s it was sold off and has since reverted back to a house.

The Star public house.

The Fox & Hounds public house.

The large old vicarage house stood next to the 'Horse and Groom'. The front of the house had a Virginia Creeper all over it which was bright red in the autumn, it was a really colourful sight. In the early 1950s a Mrs Langley lived there and in the summertime she would allow the church and chapel to hold their garden fetes on the wide, long lawn, which ran right down to the river. The grounds always looked a pretty sight with the colourful flowerbeds. It was a marvellous place to hold a fete. Sadly, the old house was pulled down some time in the 1960s. The present day vicarage house stands in Green Lane, next to Church Farm field near The Baulk.

As shown in Chapter 2, between the late 1800s and early 1900s, Clapham was a thriving village with many local industries. Alas, all seem to have gone – sign of the times – there is no longer any call for a blacksmith, a wheelwright or a shoe-tree maker, nor for boot and shoe repairers, bakers and a coffin maker. Also most of the farms who employed many of the local people, have gone; many of the fields now covered in houses.

Thomas á Becket church and churchyard, Clapham.

In the 1950s and '60s the M.O.D. had a great influence on Clapham and was probably one of the largest employers around Bedfordshire, employing many people at the R.A.E. With it came new estates of house building.

Clapham had many shops at one time, especially in the late 1960s through to the late 1980s. It had two butchers shops, a greengrocery, shoe shop as well a grocery shop, turf accountant, newsagent/sweet shop, a branch of the Midland Bank, a hardware shop and two fish and chip shops, one of them also sold wet fish.

Clapham is still served well with the shops that are left, although the Parade is dominated by three takeaways. It does have a Woolwich Building Society, a chemist, a florist, a car accessory shop and a bread/cake shop which also serves coffee and sandwiches. There are three grocery shops in the village and at the time of writing, Clapham still has a Post Office, a luxury many villages are quickly losing. When one looks back, one has to wonder why the other shops have gone. Most of the blame can be put on the motor car. People are getting about more and are able to go to the supermarkets and get their shopping in one go and bring it home in the car.

The main A6 cuts the village in half on either side of it and Clapham is just a pass-through village and not the community it once was years ago, although it does have a village primary school (built on the site of Church Farm House), a school for seniors which meets once a week in the chapel hall and a thriving Clapham Historical Society, started by Mrs Mollie Foster, daughter

The Old Vicarage next the the Horse & Groom PH. The Vicarage has since been demolished and new houses built on the site.

of the late Edward Stratford, who was the dairy farmer at the former Park Farm.

The river Ouse flows past the village and was once an important source of water for the farmers' stock when the ponds dried up before the mains water was laid on. It has flooded the village several times over the years, some of the worst flooding was in 1928, 1947 and 1998. There was minor flooding in the 1950s, but not on the scale of earlier times.

Flooding in Clapham High Street, 1998.

Aerial view of the flooding in Clapham, 1998.

What has Clapham got to look forward to?

A bypass is about to be commenced. It was first mooted in the 1930s but put to one side. What effect will this have on Clapham? It is difficult to say. I doubt that Clapham residents will use it to get to Bedford, only those from Oakley, Bletsoe and further down the A6 from Rushden. With the road scheduled to come out on top of the hill next to Sainsbury's, I can visualise even more congestion than there is already at this point.

With 200-300 more houses about to be built opposite Clapham Hospital, the roads will be more of a nightmare. How I would love to jump into a time machine and travel back to visit my namesake, John Pickering, who died in 1875, and his parents Richard and Sarah, married in 1791, who first started me on my quest to find out more about the village in which I was born – Clapham, Bedfordshire.

End